Writeriffic

Creativity Training For Writers

Here's what they're saying

about your mentor, Eva Shaw:

Sabrina, from Boston, Massachusetts, writes: Eva, you are the goddess of writers!!! (Excuse all the exclamation points.) Your encouragement and writing techniques have changed my life!! Thank you!

Lindy, from Dallas, Texas, writes: Dr. Shaw, the class was great. I think of most value to me was learning to write a decent query. I've been doing it for some time now but you caused a light to come on. I understand how it should be done. I sent another five queries out yesterday and one article. Two more articles are going out Monday and I am supposed to talk to an editor at *Better Homes & Gardens* by telephone on Monday. (She asked me to call as the result of a query… I spoke to her assistant today.) Things are really looking up for me and hopefully by the time I retire in five years my writing can supplement my police retirement. Thanks again for your patience with all my questions. Be well, happy, and successful.

Celeste, from Langley, Washington, writes: Eva clarifies, simplifies, and tosses in generous portions of wisdom and vibrant enthusiasm as she shares her techniques for unlocking the fountain of possibilities for your writing. If writing is something you value, Writeriffic is sure to add up to real benefits. Try out Eva's tips, I do! – Celeste Mergens, writer and director, Whidbey Island Writers' Conference

Rich, from Sacramento, California, writes: I highly recommend Eva's courses. Eva has never been negative, and abhors those whom she deems "Dream Smashers." These are people, any people, who for some reason criticize and insist on being negative and bringing out the negative in all and everyone they contact. We need to avoid these folks. Hey, she's turning me from an introverted hermit into an introverted writer. How cool can a teacher be? If there's a writer inside you, I think Eva can help to bring that writer to the surface.

Kathleen, from Olympia, Washington, writes: Eva Shaw is an "E ticket" ride every writer should experience. Her energy, encouragement, and enthusiasm are, without a doubt, invaluable tools to your craft, sending you into thrilling areas of creativity you can't imagine. Fasten your seat belt, and enjoy. – Kathleen Shaputis, author of Grandma Online: A Grandmother's Guide to the Internet

Ellen, from Roswell, Georgia, writes: The minute you introduce yourself in one of Eva's classes, she becomes your mentor and personal cheerleader. She genuinely cares about her students' writing ambitions, and it shows in her enthusiasm and willingness to share all that she's experienced and learned throughout the years. Combine this with the fact that she allows no negatives, adds generous dollops of warmth and humor, and you have a typical Eva Shaw class. Refreshing, exciting, and oh so satisfying.

Dennis, from Seattle, Washington, writes: Eva, I want to thank you for a very helpful and interesting class. I must say you have a wonderful way of building us up before you offer constructive criticism. By doing so we have the enthusiasm to go forward with confidence. By offering valuable suggestions we learn, yet if we incorporate your suggestions, imagine how really good our writing will become. You have a real gift for running a positive and instructive class.

B.G., from Little Rock, Arkansas, writes: Tell me it isn't over. This is the fourth online class that I have taken. In the other three, all Internet, I rarely entered the discussion areas and did not care to read what the other students had to say. With you as my instructor and mentor, I devoured every single word of this class. You made it feel like I really was in a classroom of warm human friendly bodies. Thanks go to Eva for all of the support and answers to so many questions. Thank you for the hands-on approach and the love you have for people, writing, and words. It comes through in how you approach all aspects of your life. Looking forward to the next adventure in writing with you.

Kathy, from Memphis, Tennessee, writes: This was my first online class and I loved it. Thank you for being so supportive, and Eva for just being you! God bless you!

Writeriffic

Creativity Training For Writers

Eva Shaw Ph.D.

Writeriffic Publishing Group
760-434-6445, 866-244-9047 (orders)
P. O. Box 524
Carlsbad, CA 92018-0524
www.writeriffic.com

Cover design, interior design/typesetting: Matt Shaw
Typographic specifications: Text in Times Roman, headings in PixieFont
Photo credit: CeCe Canton

Printed in the United States of America

Publisher's Cataloging-in-Publication
(Provided by Quality Books, Inc.)

Shaw, Eva, 1947-
  Writeriffic : creativity training for writers/by
Eva Shaw. – lst ed.
  p. cm.
  LCCN: 2001093307
  ISBN: 0-9705758-1-5

  1.Authorship. 2.Creation (Literary, artistic,
etc.) I. Title.

PN145.S53 2001   808'.02
                        QBI01-201019

Table of Contents

Meet Your Mentor

Eva Shaw, Ph.D.

Look for the word prolific in a dictionary and one of the definitions will be Eva Shaw. Check best selling and award winning, too. You'll see Eva's name there as well.

As an author and ghostwriter, she has produced more than sixty books, which have garnered rave reviews and won prestigious awards. Her articles have appeared in those national magazines you see at the supermarket and scores of others. At last count, she has written more than one thousand articles. With this impressive publishing record, some writers might slow down. Not Eva. New books are underway and articles are being published monthly.

Eva is a lively, engaging, and highly sought-out speaker. At conferences and events throughout the United States, her presentations draw standing-room-only crowds who seek her advice on writing and publishing. Unlike other well-published writers, Eva happily shares the tricks of the trade and how you, too, can become as abundantly creative. With the sure-fire steps she outlines, every writer can be published.

Check the endorsements in this book. Your peers praise this gifted writing teacher. Thousands have taken her writing classes and they are living their dreams. They are published writers because they have taken Eva's advice, read her books on writing, and enrolled in her courses.

Eva teaches writing with Education To Go, www.ed2go.com, and her unbeatable online classes are so popular that they are offered at 800 colleges and universities worldwide. The courses are: Travel Writing, The Craft of Magazine Writing, Writing Your Life Story, and the highly popular Writeriffic: Creativity Training for Writers.

How to Use Writeriffic

Would an athlete enter a marathon without first becoming fit? Would a hopeful singer head to a once-in-a-lifetime audition without taking voice lessons? What about an emerging writer?

Are you trying to jump into the writing world without training? How prepared are you for the competitive world of writing?

To be inventive and increase creativity, we need to write and train in order for our skills to be sharpened. That's what this book is about. It's filled with tips on creativity and training exercises to improve your creative work and even help get you over that bugaboo writer's block.

In this book you'll find trade secrets and bits of advice that I've learned in my twenty-five years as a professional writer and in the last ten years teaching thousands of emerging writers how to write. You'll discover in these pages:

- How to increase self-confidence.

- How to boost your creative gifts.

- How to capture your writer's voice and make it sing.

- How to create a creative lifestyle that promotes innovation.

- How to overcome the fear of starting.

- How to know you have what it takes to be a writer.

- And scores of writing tricks.

Every person who is given the support and opportunity can become a more creative writer. But often we do not have that support at home or from our loved ones or close friends. That's why I've created the Writeriffic exercises. That's why I hope you'll consider me your mentor.

This book and exercises are guaranteed to boost your creativity. If, after you do them for a month, you do not truly believe that your skills as a writer have improved, you have my permission to write or e-mail and complain.

When you flip through this book, you might initially think that the exercises are too easy. Do not be fooled. They are deceptively simple. The exercises will take you five minutes or five hours. It's up to you. Most of the exercises include variations that can become a part of a long-term creativity program. Yes, you have the potential right in your hands to create a once-a-day writing program that could last a year or more.

Turn to the exercises and look at the blank pages next to them. You'll use these to complete the exercises. See the words, "Continued on ____" at the bottom of each page? Should you need more than one page to complete the exercise, there are pages at the back of the book. Simply fill in the appropriate page number and you can instantly find the continuation of your writing.

Some of the exercises were created strictly for this book. Others have sparked creativity in thousands of my writing students who have been in my traditional university classes, attended workshops at conferences, and enrolled in the online classes I conduct at colleges and universities worldwide, through Education to Go. I have seen how powerful the exercises are… and how fun, yet challenging, they can be.

That's it. Use this book. Make it your new best friend and it will be. Good writing.

Writeriffic and You
Styling Your Creative Life

Have you ever stared at a blank computer screen or a sheet of paper? Did it glare back at you? Challenge you? Intimidate you? Have you ever wondered what you could or should write? Have you ever stopped writing?

You could be suffering from page fright, often worse than writer's block, because we must face a blank page in order to capture our dreams. I've heard that some creative people who look at the computer screen or the end of a pencil and feel unable to start or continue to write consider page fright chronic. Some writers joke that it's deadly. I've seen it stall some promising careers.

Have you heard of page fright before or ever had a touch of it? Most writers have. So if you've just said yes, you're in good company. I have been troubled by the ailment more than once in my writing career. I've learned ways to get over it. You can do it too, once you have the tools. Then you can become the creative, resourceful, happy, and clever novelist, nonfiction writer, short-story writer, storyteller, poet, screenwriter, or playwright you've dreamed of becoming.

Before you let page fright trip you, consider the other things that might be going on in your life that may be stopping you from writing. This doesn't mean you're a failure by any stretch of the imagination. It assures me that you're a bona fide human being.

Let's say that you've been given a critical project that's going to demand hours of overtime, the kids or pets or parents are at a troubling time in their lives, the car made a weird noise on the way to the office, and your throat feels scratchy. Yes, I've had those years myself. That's where these exercises can be a life saver, a creative port in the storm. Even on the most hectic of days, when chaos fills the air, you can do one or two of the exercises and know that you're honing your writing and creative skills.

If a block hits, look at what's happening in your non-writing life, your work life, and your relationships. Are you getting enough sleep? Do you need to talk with your doctor or a listening friend? Is it time to sharpen your computer skills or learn researching techniques? There could be lots of reasons why you're suffering, and they all could be because life sometimes gets in our way.

For the next few minutes, pretend a large box with a sturdy lid is sitting next to you. Take the lid off and imagine you're jamming in all your favorite reasons and problems and excuses for not writing. You can even pretend that a complaining loved one, a boss, or a coworker is going inside. Put in the ones about being a "bad" writer, not having a degree in journalism, or being forced to write without a rich relative to support you while you concentrate on creativity.

Now slam that lid closed. Put a heavy book on top if that makes the box more secure. Don't let those problems or excuses out for the next six weeks or while you're doing the Writeriffic exercises. If you ever want them, they'll be there. Actually, after you've finished the exercises you might try those problems on for size. I have a hunch that you won't want them anymore as accessories to your creative life.

Don't you feel more creative already?

Now that you're open to a more creative life, let's talk about the nature of creativity. Forget what someone once wrote or said about good writers having to "open a vein." Sorry, I'm not willing to bleed for my work and would never expect you to either. Besides that concept is downright messy.

Suffering For My Art?
Not Me

Forget what you might have heard about writers having to "suffer for their art." That's a myth. You can be a regular guy or gal, love writing, and write well. Your diploma might be from the School of Experience. Regardless of your age or your background, you can be a published writer.

I must admit that once you catch the exhilaration, the pure bliss of creativity and writing, you'll become addicted. But don't worry. This addiction is good for you.

Creativity is as invigorating as a walk through the countryside on a perfect spring day. Creativity is like winning an unexpected prize, getting into those jeans you wore in high school, being told that your house or car is worth twice as much as when you bought it years ago, and seeing a toddler take a first step. Creativity is these feelings all rolled into one.

You may already be writing or have a desire to write fiction — to tell stories for novels or short stories. You may be composing poetry, concocting images that are thoughtful and dazzling. You may be writing articles or nonfiction books and need to enliven the text to make it irresistible. Or you may be thinking of writing the stories of your life or the lives of those folks you love.

Yet, you may also realize that your creative skills aren't as good as you would like. That's not being negative, but smart. Like the training athletes and singers require, which we mentioned in the beginning, writing takes practice and practice takes time.

Did you just think, "How does Eva know this?" I've made choices in my own career to design and live a creative life, and without a doubt I know there's a more creative life waiting for you. But you must take that first step. You must read this book and do the exercises. When you do, you'll never look back and wonder, "Could I have been a good writer?" You'll be a good writer, with practice.

Being a creative writer means you need to honor your creative feelings. You'll need to pull ideas from deep inside or straight from this morning's newspaper.

Creativity means you need to filter or sift through the thoughts coming from your head and the everyday world. Creative writers examine their ideas with their hearts as well as their heads. Yes, this take practice, but please be assured that you can do it.

Your Inner Writer

I'm often asked: Is it possible to turn our creative visions, even those that haven't taken form yet, into purposeful prose? You bet — and then some.

Those who are just testing the waters of creative writing sometimes think that the ideas that come out of nowhere are silly, stupid, or worthless. Yet the more we talk to other writers, the more we realize the stuff that creativity is made of is produced from the visions in our minds. That's pretty remarkable.

Creativity is the way you translate what you hear or feel or see inside into a format that you share with the reader. For writers, creativity is ideas processed into words.

If I were a brain specialist instead of a writer, I could tell you exactly what hormones or brain connections are activated in the creative process. For me, the process doesn't matter as much as how I get those ideas onto the page. We do that with practice.

Do you remember as a youngster learning a new skill? Do you recall learning to ride a bike, play a sport, or dance a complex routine? How about when you learned to maneuver through a favorite video game? Do you remember learning to tie your shoes or shoot baskets? These skills took tenacity and a willingness to make mistakes and take risks throughout the process.

I don't know about you, but when I learned to roller-skate I wore off the skin on my knees and still got up to try again. I never once wondered whether I was going to wear those pavement-induced scars for the rest of my life. I was determined to skate with the other kids, and I did what it took. Luckily my mother had lots of adhesive bandages.

We had fun learning those skills. That's what creating is about. What feels good to your ear when reading your writing out loud, what makes your heart swell, and what simply makes sense — these become creative visions to share.

Think of writing and creativity as recess for the brain. Not every creative thought must be attached to a novel, short story, poem, essay, book, or article. Not every creative effort must be connected with writing at all. I believe that the more other creative activities you participate in, from painting a barn to painting a picture, the more creative you become and the better your writing will be. You might say that doing any creative activity supports your inner writer.

Right now, take a moment to figure out ways to add more creativity to your world. I love to garden, and if you were to visit my yard right now you would see I'm a creative gardener. When I'm working on a knotty piece of plotting or mulling over research for a nonfiction book, I head for the garden to cut, shovel, and water. Novelist Irving Stone said, "When I have trouble writing, I step outside my studio into the garden and pull weeds until my mind clears — I find weeding to be the best therapy there is for writer's block." No matter what you've heard, it's simply not true that I allow the weeds to grow so I can pull them when I'm having a writing problem.

Here's a start-up list of creative activities to get you going. Notice that they have nothing to do with writing. Make it your goal to add at least one of these activities to your week. Better yet, add one to each day.

- Weaving
- Model making
- Working (in an enjoyable way) on the car
- Craft making
- Playing a musical instrument
- Woodworking and building
- Sewing or other needlecrafts
- Gardening
- Attending a book signing or literary event
- Going to the theater
- Painting
- Yarn crafting
- Singing
- Working with clay
- Baking
- Dancing
- Cooking (but only if you love it)
- Doing puzzles
- Practicing yoga or a stretching routine
- Doodling
- Walking, running, swimming, cycling.

As you add more creativity to your life, you will become a more creative writer. It sounds simple because it is.

Writing and Your Life

Creativity, to be channeled into writing, must have a direction. You can set up official-sounding goals and objectives, but all I'm asking is that you write every day.

Just ten minutes, or the time it takes to do one of the Writeriffic writing exercises. Don't worry if your writing feels stiff. It's okay. By the time you've written on all the pages in this book, your creative muscles will be strong and powerful.

Moreover, are you aware that if you start today and write one page every day for just one year, you'll have a piece of work that is 365 pages long? Now let's flip that coin. What if you don't write? Next year, you'll still be thinking that you want to write but have nothing to show for it. Pretty sad picture, isn't it?

Write every day regardless of how you feel or what's going on in your life. Set the kitchen timer or the alarm on your watch. Sit there for five minutes (or longer, depending on your schedule). Do this twice a day or for the entire ten minutes in one sitting.

Start here in this journal. Make it your best friend. Take it to lunch. Seriously, drag it along when you're going on break, heading on a trip, taking a holiday, lounging at the beach, sitting in the garden.

In six weeks, you'll have proof that you're a better writer.

Your Writer's Voice

Have you read or heard the poems and short stories by the American writer Edgar Allan Poe? His writer's voice is lyrical and can be downright scary. Poe was a master at conjuring up frightening images. The bleakness tumbled out of his prose.

Now contrast the writer's voice of Poe with that of another American writer, Pulitzer Prize winning humorist Dave Barry. These examples are at opposite ends of the writing spectrum. If you are familiar with their prose, you would never mistake one for another. These men have distinctive writing voices. You do too.

The idea of a writer's voice may be a new concept to you or one you're hoping to capture. A writer's voice is the way thoughts and creativity weave together. It's the way you alone impart information, knowledge, entertainment, or inspiration.

Keep in mind that the writer's voice you create initially will probably change through the years. When I go back and read some of the articles and short stories I wrote for publication in the early 1980s, the writing seems formal, bulky, like a heavy wool overcoat.

Times have changed along with my writer's voice. Today the words I choose are simpler. When I first started my professional writing career more than twenty years ago, I worked hard to find big words. Somehow, I thought that if I wrote using words I'd never use in a conversation, someone (namely an editor) would think I was brainy and would consequently buy my work. To some extent, this approach might have worked because I did get published, but I've learned a great lesson since then. There are more people who enjoy reading material that uses everyday words than people who like to read books and articles that force them to look up words in a dictionary.

Now my writing is casual. By casual I don't mean careless. It doesn't mean I can string together phrases and unintelligent words hoping someone will say, "Wow, that has a deep meaning." Trust me, if readers don't get what I'm saying right off the bat, I've failed as a writer — as a translator of images to the brain.

The casual writing voice I enjoy writing and reading is everywhere. Today's writing supplies information and entertainment in an easy-to-understand form. The current style is along the lines of the language you find in the newspaper and hear on television and the radio.

Many writing teachers suggest that those who are new to the creative field shouldn't try to discover a writing voice. "Hogwash," I say. Cultivating a voice, listening for subtle changes, and then finding a voice is an incredibly exciting part of the creative process.

No real writer can ignore the drive to create. As we write, we hear our words and examine the images that are created. I believe these words and images bring our writing voices to life. Why put off this adventure for some time in the future when you can start now?

Your writing voice will evolve just as mine has. But to evolve you must begin to hear yours. To do that you must write. I always recommend to emerging and advanced writers that they read their work out loud. I started to do it years ago when I was writing radio scripts. I figured, quite simply, that if I read the material out loud and I tumbled over a phrase, the show's host, who was reading my words, would most likely do the same. Not a good thing if I needed that job, which I did. Even today, I still use this tool to improve the readability of my work.

Take a few minutes in the next week and read the works of your favorite writers. Read the words out loud. As you read, make some actual or mental notes about how characters are described or how information is provided. Consider, too, how the writer creates the images or examples. Is the writer effective? If not, why not? What specifically do you like about the writer's work? There are no right or wrong answers.

By reading the work of published writers and discovering what we like and dislike, we can then put these techniques to work in our own writing.

To train your ear to identify writers' voices, rewrite (either on paper or by reading it out loud) the following paragraph in the way you imagine it would be written by Amy Tan, Danielle Steel, Barbara Kingsolver, Stephen King, Louis L'Amour, Shel Silverstein, Dr. Seuss, Erma Bombeck, Irving Stone, Jackie Collins, or Maya Angelou. If you prefer, rewrite it in the voice of Shakespeare, Steinbeck, or Shelley.

Here you go. Have fun.

> The woman tapped her fingers on the edge of the novel. Midnight and still the phone stayed silent. Could she have been sleeping and missed it? She checked for a flickering light on the answering machine. Nothing. "Call the second you get to Los Angeles," she'd told them. But did they listen? "Parents today," she said. "You just can't trust them out of your sight."

If a romance writer, such as Danielle Steel, had written that paragraph, the main character might be named Salina Lasiandra or Belinda Belo. Could you see this character stomping her little foot in annoyance? Or flicking a fiery red curl behind her ear and then squaring her chin? Why, if I were to create this story in Danielle Steel's voice, the character might even smile with her ripe, kissable lips.

Stephen King's voice would present the images with a hint of menace. Or everything would be too normal and then disaster would strike. There might be a weather report predicting freak tornadoes. Or the main character would suffer from recurring visions of hijacking and terrorists.

Now go back to that paragraph and create it in your own writer's voice. What you may hear is creativity working to produce a uniqueness that is you alone.

As you work on the Writeriffic exercises, don't try to push your writer's voice. It must evolve, and evolution takes time.

An Inspired Existence Made Easier

Writers, athletes, and actors have a lot in common. Most writers have rituals that we follow to help us cope with the nervous tension that can come before, during, or even after a writing project is finished. To get on the stage or the playing field, or hit the Save key and keep your writing, you may have to go through specific actions.

I've found it intriguing that most writers, including those whose names are on the lists of best-selling books, have rituals they must do before starting. One writer I know must complete six pages of a novel before she stops for the day, but before she gets this far, she has a cup of tea on her patio, reads the paper (comics first), and then takes a long walk.

Another writer likes to get the house in shape before he starts writing. He does the chores, packs lunches for the kids, and waves good-bye to his spouse before knuckling down to the keyboard and his weekly column. "If I don't do all these, I feel guilty," he says, "and my writing is stiff."

A third author starts the writing day by sitting in front of her computer, before turning it on, to ask God for direction in her writing ministry.

I'd like to suggest a ritual I've found helpful. Once I hit the Start button on the computer, I begin my day by saying thank you to someone for something. Although these days I often use e-mail to write notes, I frequently make time to write and send a pretty card. We all love getting postal mail — most of the time the carrier just delivers bills.

Sometimes I'm asked how I have so many people to thank. The card or e-note is really an excuse to get my creative juices flowing and my brain back to thinking in words. I thank family for just being there, friends for putting up with my creative jaunts into whimsy or worse, editors for being kind to my work, agents for responding to my e-mail, colleagues for listening to my newest, craziest schemes. I also write fan letters to my favorite authors, and many of them reply.

Thanking others is a positive, productive way to start a writing time. If you have yet to find a routine, a ritual, for yourself, I recommend this one.

Don't think you're strange if you must go through a specific set of movements or rituals before settling down to write. Have you ever seen an actor do deep breathing exercises or a singer warm up her or his voice? What of the athletes? We've all seen them pull an ear, yank on a jersey, or touch a good luck charm. If any of these things work for you, you'll be in good company with others in competitive and creative fields.

Creative Kick Starts

Do you know it's okay to not clean up your desk and put everything in order at the end of your writing time?

Have you ever stopped writing mid-sentence when you're finished for the day?

These techniques could increase your creativity. Contrary to what some ultra-organized folks think, adding these two techniques to your creative writing tool belt may make a difference in your productivity. I call these Creative Kick Starts.

"Why?" "How come?" I can almost hear you ask. It's simple.

Those who follow this practice have an edge because when they return, they just pick up where they left off. This is a technique I use all the time, so if you should visit my office don't just assume I'm messy. The clutter is planned. I don't organize and really clean up until the project on which I'm working is finished.

Using this technique you really don't stop for the day or stop the writing project. You're just taking a break from it, so it's easier to begin again.

You can also reduce the hurdle of starting any writing project once you realize that many writers share the same fear. We ask ourselves:

What if I can't complete the short story?

What if a reviewer doesn't like my work?

What if I'm not good enough to write another cookbook?

If you could listen inside the fear area of a writer's brain, you would probably hear one of these.

You would hear the fears in my mind, too. Every single time I begin a new writing project, I have a period of worry, misgiving, and, okay, alarm. What if, after sixty plus books and more than a thousand magazine articles, I really can't research, can't compose a sentence, can't finish what I've been contracted to do? Horror of horrors, what if I suddenly can't write?

That's the worry I go through. At one time, fear paralyzed me for weeks. Then with plenty of self-talk (encouraging words spoken out loud and in a commanding voice), I got going. Of course, everything was fine, but it was scary nonetheless.

Now when page fright appears, I realize that the feeling of fear is part of my creative process. If you have it, remember it doesn't mean you're a failure or a bad writer — it means you're normal with normal anxieties.

Can You Make It as a Writer?

Can you make it as a writer? This is a huge question and one you may have been wrestling with for some time, maybe even years. It could be that your spouse, kids, parents, and co-workers are longing to ask the question but haven't yet.

The truth is that anyone with tenacity and a measure of creativity can become a good writer and a published writer. If you are a survivor, an overachiever, and a worrywart, you'll be even more likely to be successful. (That's advice from your fellow surviving, overachieving, worrying mentor.)

How can you make your career "happen"? If you weren't born into a family that owns a huge publishing conglomerate, then you do the work and hone your craft. You become a wordsmith. How much work? Whatever it takes. But first answer this question: Are you happy, exhilarated, challenged, and determined when writing? If you answered yes, then you would be crazy to give up something that makes you feel this way.

Today, sharing your work with other writers in a critique group is considered cool. If that's true, I'm not cool, and I'd like you to consider being un-cool with me. Sharing work too soon can destroy the creative process. I can better use the time I would spend in a group by actually doing what I do best — writing. This is especially true if, like me, you have family, home, church, and other work obligations.

Instead, learn the craft and take classes (online, on campus, and at conferences). If you have negative people in your life, or perhaps you've started to write before but became detoured, simply don't mention what you're doing. Okay, tell your spouse or partner, but keep writing for yourself until you're ready. You'll know when.

Ignore anyone who says, "You've got to be born with it." With practice, you'll improve. Sure you could fail, but as that great philosopher Wayne Gretzky said, "You miss 100 percent of the shots you don't take." Here's a plan.

1. Write every day, in this book. Do it during lunch break or while waiting for the kids.

2. Read books by writers on writing. My favorites are my own books on writing, *Writing the Nonfiction Book* and *The Successful Writer's Guide to Publishing Magazine Articles*, *The Courage to Write* by Keyes, *On Writing Well* by Zinsser, and *Self-Editing for Fiction Writers* by Browne and King. These books are written in plain English for us plain English types.

3. Give yourself time to evolve. Odds are you crawled before you walked and definitely walked before you ran.

Now here's the final part. Look in the mirror. Smile. That's a writer facing you. Can you see it in the eyes? Could you tell this person that writing is all a bunch of foolishness? Not if you're honest.

Really now, what alternative do you have? If you have the heart to write, you must.

Time to Create
The Writeriffic Writing Exercises

Here are your creativity exercises. I promise you they will increase your skill as a creative writer, but only if you do them. As my mama said, "Talk is cheap." If you have only talked about writing up to now, stop that talk and start to write.

Some of the exercises have variations, so there are really enough of them to last a year. You might want to write on extra paper and then copy your writing onto the pages following each exercise in this journal. I hope you'll write directly into this book so you can see how your voice gains power and evolves.

The extra pages at the back of this book are for your creative variations on the exercises. Don't write for your high school teacher. He or she will never see this creative work, so you're safe. Further, the Grammar and Spelling Police do not walk this beat. Have fun. Take risks. Just create.

When you have done all the exercises, heard your writer's voice, and felt your creative energies surging, contact me. I want to hear about the hurdles that you've climbed over and the successes you've had. I want to know what works for you and what doesn't. I want to know about other creativity exercises you've used. I want to be your mentor.

Send notes to askeva@evashaw.com or P. O. Box 524, Carlsbad, CA 92018-0524. I'm looking forward to it and I'll reply too.

Writing Exercise
Eighteen

Draw the number 18 on the top of the next available page. Now before picking up a pen, think about who you were at this age. Your eighteenth birthday was a rite of passage (if you're younger than eighteen, select a birthday that has special meaning). You might want to focus on your birthday party, high school graduation, or being on the edge of adulthood. Many of us were married, left home, took a first job, entered college, or went to war by the time we were eighteen years old. Eighteen leaves a mark on us like no other birthday.

Fill the following page with your thoughts or perhaps a poem.

There's no right or wrong way to do this exercise, but you must recapture some of the feeling of that time in your life.

Possibilities: Write about the music, food, clothing, slang, styles, hobbies, family, parties, high school, or friends that affected you.

Look within yourself for the feelings and motivators you use in fictional characters.

Use the extra pages in the back of the journal to write about other milestone birthdays or events in your life.

*Continued on page*_____

Writing Exercise
Finish the Story

Select one of the phrases below and fill the next page with your story. Be creative. Want an extra challenge? Use dialogue or develop a twist for the ending.

It had been a long day that got even longer when…

Town folks liked us well enough until they met my Aunt Fran and her pet…

January couldn't come fast enough when I heard…

"Don't ever let her know you have that information," he whispered to…

That was the last time Chris mentioned the "incident" until…

It's said that fools rush in where angels fear to tread, but even fools wouldn't have…

"Darling, no one will find out," CJ assured…

Some stains come out, but blood…

Pat and Maude worked in silence as they…

Conversation stopped as Elmo arrived with…

You might want to sketch some ideas before you begin writing. With so many stories to finish and so many genres to choose from, you can do a variation of this exercise every day for a month.

*Continued on page*_____

Writing Exercise
Don't Get Arrested

Go to your favorite public place, such as McDonalds, the airport, a city park, or the library. Shopping malls, soccer games, and the office lunchroom are excellent places to do this exercise. You now have a literary license to people watch and eavesdrop.

Take along a pad and pencil, and, as you eat, watch other people. Make notes of facial features, laughs, body movements. You need to know how people talk, walk, and eat so that you can put this information into your writing.

Be subtle because the nice police officer who questions your behavior will not believe that this is a creativity exercise you're doing to improve your writing. Don't stalk people. If they move away, select another person.

Now seriously, choose a person or make a composite from those you've taken notes on and create a story about this individual. Kids, teens, and seniors are often the best people to observe because they're less cautious with their behavior.

Now create a short story about a person or a situation. Create a mystery or a secret and twist it around. Think "what if." Let's say you're watching a child with an adult. Most noncreative folks would see a grandmother and her precious granddaughter. But if you think "what if," you could see an alien attempting to abduct a senior citizen. Now you've got the idea.

Write enough to fill up the following page.

*Continued on page*_____

Writing Exercise
The Peanut-Butter Writer

Write about your favorite way to eat peanut butter. This is fun to do in poetry, too. Use the adjoining page.

Hate peanut butter? Select another food. Actually you can use the extra pages at the back of this book and write about a different food every day for a week or a month or a year.

Some of my writing students, especially those who are blocked, do this as a morning warm-up exercise. I've read "An Ode to a Bagel" and "Once Upon An Omelet."

*Continued on page*_____

Writing Exercise
He Said, She Said

Write a short story with a beginning, middle, and end, using dialogue only, and fill up the next page. Before you begin, list the events. Start off with a bang, figuratively at least. Here's what one story might look like:

"Don't point that at me."

"Mother, it's a water pistol."

"I don't give a fig, Susie. I've seen them on TV. It's a Super Slosher."

"And I even got two for the same price."

"Now we're cooking. Oh, sorry, honey, I didn't know this thing was loaded."

Never once were you told that this is a conversation between parent and child, but that quickly came out in the dialogue. Make that your goal.

Continued on page_____

Writing Exercise
Object of Writing

Select one object that is connected with your life. It might be a locket that belonged to your grandmother. It might be the family Bible. It might be your father's police badge, a friend's house key, a favorite novel, a childhood toy, or an animal companion's collar or leash.

Study the object for at least five minutes. If appropriate, you might want to carry the object in your pocket for the next few hours or even sleep with it beneath your pillow. Sound odd? All creativity is innovative and, if these ideas feel right, then they are.

It's a requirement that you sit quietly and touch, smell, feel, and study the object for at least five minutes. If necessary, set an alarm so you don't budge until the time's up.

Once you're comfortable with the ideas and object, begin to write on the next page. You need not make complete sentences and might want to write a haiku or poem.

*Continued on page*_____

Writing Exercise
Learned It Myself

Write about something you taught yourself how to do. I've read essays on everything from tying shoes to learning to live alone after the untimely death of a young spouse.

Tell why you wanted to learn it in the first place. Describe how you went about learning it. Explain what you learned from the process. Make sure you include why or how learning this thing affected you.

Be sure to give it a title, so leave the top line blank on the adjoining page until you've finished writing.

Continued on page_____

Writing Exercise
All Natural

Write for five minutes or until you fill the following page on some aspect of nature — perhaps a cloud, maybe the wind, or even a fallen leaf. Write poetry, write fragmented sentences, or draw a sketch in this journal.

There are so many variations on this exercise that you could spend a year or more writing about nature. Longfellow, Thoreau, and Muir all did.

*Continued on page*_____

Writing Exercise
Wordy Fun

Go to a dictionary. Open it at random. Allow your finger to run down the page and stop at will. I like to do this with my eyes closed. Select a word, read the definitions, and then write a short story using some or all of the forms of the word.

Write to fill a page of this journal. Don't think too much. Just play with words.

If you enjoy this exercise, you might want to use it to start out every writing session. The possibilities are unlimited, and imagine what a whiz you'll be at Scrabble, too.

*Continued on page*_____

Writing Exercise
Picture This

Take a picture out of your family photo album. Find one in which you are prominent and, preferably, one of you as a child or younger.

Are you standing with a sibling or family member? Maybe it's a class photo where all the kids look bright and scrubbed.

Perhaps you've taken a picture from a birthday party. There you are with your grandparents hovering in the background. Maybe you're a teenager and posed against your new car, a banged up Ford that you thought was hot stuff.

Study the photo for about five minutes. Set the timer if you think you'll have trouble with this part of the exercise. Use the photograph as a vehicle to time travel back to the memory of that exact day.

Here's what to look for:

◉ Background — Grass, dirt, house, a city street.

◉ Facial expressions — Upset, happy, faking a smile, naïve, frustrated, silly.

◉ Clothing — Casual, torn, mismatched, party clothes.

◉ Season — Just before the first day of school, stuffed into a hand-me-down snow suit.

◉ Location — Kitchen table, Yosemite National Park, Aunt Millie's fishing pond.

◉ Accessories — Toys, dolls, sporting equipment.

◉ Details — Bandages on a skinned knee, a terrible haircut, the cat curling around your ankles, the dog pulling on your swimsuit.

Make some notes on paper or on the computer. Continue to look at the picture. Feel the moment.

Trust me, you'll remember everything once you stare hard enough at the photograph. Don't be surprised if you once again feel anger, hurt, or bliss. These are some of the emotions you'll want to use when you're writing your life story or creating characters for that novel.

You may even want to clear your mind and close your eyes for a few moments before you begin. It helps to relax and maybe meditate so you can relive some of the emotions you experienced at that time in your life. Make some more notes about how you will write the photo essay, but don't start yet.

Need ideas? You can tell about the day, what happened, what didn't happen, why you were there, or how it feels to see yourself as a child.

Although I don't remember the day, because I was just two at the time, one of my favorite pictures is of my sisters and me. We're lined up on a shabby sofa that had been covered with a granny-square afghan. My grandmother Paulina crocheted it during the Great Depression. Because my grandmother couldn't afford new yarn, the afghan was made by unraveling cast-off sweaters, a practice that today seems as foreign as traveling in covered wagons.

Because I've memorized the stories behind the photographs in our family album, I know this one was taken the day before we left New Jersey, just after my younger sister was born. I look at those three little girls and marvel at my parents' bravery or foolishness to trek along old Route 66 to California with three tiny kids, one of whom was just days old.

Then in my mind's eye, I see the three of us as adults and wonder what life might have been like if we had grown up along the shore in New Jersey, near over-protective grandparents and the traditions that had stifled my parents. I feel sorrow because a few years ago my younger sister lost her battle with cancer. I feel joy to be close to my older sister although we're separated by hundreds of miles. And I'm nearly teary-eyed looking at that afghan that now has an honored place in my own living room.

Those are my feelings and thoughts based on a photo.

Now write yours. Use the following page. Here again, you might want to jot down some ideas or ponder the assignment before you begin.

This assignment has many variations and the possibilities are only limited by your supply of old photos.

*Continued on page*_____

Writing Exercise
Lions and Tigers and Bears, Oh My

Flip through some magazines and find one picture of a person and another of an animal. *National Geographic* magazine is a great place to find animal pictures. Cut out the figures and place them together so that you have the body of a human and the head of a creature. You might connect a photo of a fashion model to a sea turtle. You may want to blend the body of a baseball player with the head of a peacock.

Spend five minutes contemplating the personality of this new being. When you're ready, create a plot with this character as the protagonist, the star of your story, right here in your journal.

Continued on page_____

Writing Exercise
Read All About It

Get a copy of your city or town's newspaper, the print or the electronic version. Select one article from the front page. Read it thoroughly and then put it away for a few hours or even overnight. Now read it again and see what creative thoughts are stirred. Your goal here is to write a story based on some aspect of the article.

Fictionalize all you want, or rewrite the event as an informational article or essay. This exercise should fill up the following page. However, why not make it last for a year? You can repeat it every day when you open the morning paper.

*Continued on page*_____

Writing Exercise
Seek It, Find It, Write It

Go into your purse, wallet, or that spot in your house or office where you keep stuff that really has no other place but that you can't throw away. In my house, it has always been called the junk drawer. Take three items out and place them on the table in front of you. Ponder them for a while; then choose one to write about.

As you write a poem, story, or personal essay, sparked by the object you've selected, keep these points in mind:

- ◉ Stay focused on your message.

- ◉ Add thoughtful, funny, colorful examples.

- ◉ Don't tell the mundane details.

- ◉ Make the message universal to reach a wide readership.

- ◉ Arrive at a basic truth.

- ◉ Get your reader involved — ask a question.

- ◉ Use emotions and word pictures.

- ◉ Pick an experience you care about.

- ◉ Steer clear of anger and negative emotions.

- ◉ Reveal yourself.

- ◉ Use the essay to educate, inform, and entertain.

Write your essay on the following page.

Continued on page____

Writing Exercise
Power and Influence

While we like to believe we are in charge of our lives, in truth other people have a profound effect on us. Have you ever given advice to a friend or your children and suddenly you realize your parents used those very words? We've all done that.

People influence our lives. Some for the better. Others have the opposite effect. Think of someone who affected you in some way. It needn't be a life-changing experience.

Did a boss fire you from a job — a job you weren't at all suited for — and did you realize later it was for the best? Did a parent or sibling teach you a skill, such as model building, knitting, or golfing, that has brought you joy? Was there a parent or older adult whose negative role modeling helped decide your own values?

You may want to select someone who was instrumental in a significant life experience, such as a birth, graduation, wedding, death, or religious experience.

Want an extra challenge? Tie your character to an event, like an earthquake or tidal wave, or a holiday, such as Easter or Valentine's Day.

Once you've made some notes, fill up the next page. Don't rush.

Because many people affect our lives, including lovers, children, and even strangers, you can use the pages at the back of your journal to repeat this exercise many times.

*Continued on page*_____

Writing Exercise
Review It

Go online to Amazon.com or another online bookseller and write a review for a book you've enjoyed. This exercise in creativity gives you practice editing your words and honing the skill of writing for the audience of people who will read your posting.

It's lots of fun to see your name next to the online review. And it just might give you the creative boost to realize that you want your book in these bookstores, too.

Write your review on the next page before posting it online.

*Continued on page*_____

Writing Exercise
Home Sweet Home and More

In fifty words or less, describe your favorite place on the planet. Choose a place you really love. Write about your hometown or about the region where you live. You can write about the place where you took your last vacation.

Be flowery or serious, but you may not use the following words: pretty, attractive, good, nice, beautiful, lovely, or other wishy-washy descriptive words, and steer clear of very, really, especially, quite, or incredible.

*Continued on page*_____

Writing Exercise
Assemble This

Draw lines between the most unlikely combination of the following words, and then create a poem using the nouns and modifiers. You can mix and match and twist things around.

Just for fun, I've shared my poem after the list.

Nouns	Modifiers
dinosaur	unsullied
dog	tight-lipped
quiche	fluffy
hotel	dusty
golfer	plump
banana	rusted
cactus	bleached
robot	squashy
tornado	winged
éclair	downy
cone	delicate
sneakers	tiny
mustang	menacing
elevator	mind-numbing
tile	ulcerated
book	kaput
sister	petrified
bathtub	battered
Jupiter	wrestled

cobweb	sterile
shoe	spotless
pliers	untainted
coffee	mud-spattered
peanut	brawny
coverlet	encrusted
hamburger	saccharine

Here's what it might look like:

Sister soft

Petrified next to the fluffy cactus

Sneakers brawny, but battered and bleached

Heading to a sterile bathtub

Sister soft

A robot, untainted, tight-lipped and winged.

No one is expecting Pulitzer Prize winning poetry, but make your goal to increase your creativity. Use the adjoining page and the extra pages at the back to assemble more poems. This is a simple, highly creative exercise that could spark fresh ideas in all your writing.

Continued on page_____

Writing Exercise
Retell the Tale

Take a children's story, such as *Little Red Riding Hood*, and retell it in a strictly modern way. Give your story a twist, do unexpected things with details. Don't forget to show (by their behavior) the personalities of your characters; don't just tell about them.

Write to fill up the next page. Because this creativity exercise has so many variations, from Bible stories to such classics as *Little Women* and *Treasure Island*, you can use the extra pages at the back of your journal to work on a new story every day for a month or more.

*Continued on page*_____

Writing Exercise

365 or More: Make It Up, Shake It Up, Create A Story

Start at the top left grouping of words and work your way through this list. Take one group each day. Use the first word of the group as the first word of your story, and fill one page in your journal.

Use the two remaining words wherever they fit. Don't forget that every story needs a place, a plot, and something to move a plot forward.

hug	haircut	teacup	fig
linen	jalopy	alien	tornado
pirate	peanut	lavender	blossom
raven	yellow	shock	invisible
tiny	sink	terrier	baloney
laundry	gentlewoman	birdhouse	Venice
waterfall	divide	aficionado	halt
banana	purpose	postcard	ice tea
babe	volunteer	bedspread	morose
sour	sweet	apple	pencil
brittle	deodorant	leg	grin
lasagna	Paris	meander	elephant
college	taxes	dishwasher	envelope
burden	blast	pine cone	cram
black	toast	candy bar	blood

nectar	bumblebee	unemployment	unwrap
tome	teenagers	laser	chocolate
corkscrew	sneakers	staples	gargoyle
tuna	cat	bacon	dust
nephew	tabloid	cylinder	lump
pillow	pie	slink	suffocate
bazaar	petticoat	conductor	elevator
horse	pork roast	perfume	pear
monster	eraser	reindeer	toad
orphan	applause	snow	preacher
chicken	advice	smile	orange
sun	mouse	sterile	tart

*Continued on page*_____

The End as Your Beginning

When you've finished the Writeriffic exercises, please let me know. I created these exercises for you and I want your feedback. When I get your letter, I'll write back. You can write to me at askeva@evashaw.com or by writing to: P. O. Box 524, Carlsbad, CA 92018-0524.

*Continued from page*_____

*Continued from page*_____

To make it as a writer...
Read every day.

Continued from page_____

Continued from page_____

*Continued from page*_____

To make it as a writer…
Develop and maintain
a positive attitude.

Continued from page_____

_____

_____

_____

_____

_____

_____

_____

_____

_____

_____

_____

_____

_____

_____

_____

_____

_____

_____

_____

_____

_____

_____

_____

_____

_____

Continued from page_____

Continued from page_____

_____

_____

_____

_____

_____

_____

_____

_____

_____

_____

_____

_____

_____

_____

_____

_____

_____

_____

_____

_____

_____

_____

_____   To make it as a writer...

_____   Be selective with whom you

_____   share your emerging work.

_____

Continued from page_____

Continued from page_____

Continued from page_____

To make it as a writer...
Tell others you're a writer.

Continued from page_____

*Continued from page*_____

Continued from page_____

_____

_____

_____

_____

_____

_____

_____

_____

_____

_____

_____

_____

_____

_____

_____

_____

_____

_____

To make it as a writer...
Listen.

Continued from page_____

Continued from page_____

Continued from page_____

_____

_____

_____

_____

_____

_____

_____

_____

_____

_____

_____

_____

_____

_____

_____

_____

_____

_____

_____

_____

_____

_____   To make it as a writer...

_____   Take risks, try new genres.

_____

_____

Continued from page_____

_____

_____

_____

_____

_____

_____

_____

_____

_____

_____

_____

_____

_____

_____

_____

_____

_____

_____

_____

_____

_____

_____

_____

_____

_____

_____

Continued from page_____

Continued from page_____

_____

_____

_____

_____

_____

_____

_____

_____

_____

_____

_____

_____

_____

_____

_____

_____

_____

_____

_____

_____

_____

_____   To make it as a writer...
                                           Tell the truth.
_____

_____

_____

Continued from page_____

Continued from page_____

Continued from page_____

_____

_____

_____

_____

_____

_____

_____

_____

_____

_____

_____

_____

_____

_____

_____

_____

_____

_____

_____

_____

_____

_____

_____

_____   To make it as a writer...
                                        Treat others as you would
_____   like to be treated.

_____

*Continued from page*_____

Continued from page_____

Continued from page_____

_____

_____

_____

_____

_____

_____

_____

_____

_____

_____

_____

_____

_____

_____

_____

_____

_____

_____

_____   To make it as a writer...
                                        Be easy to work with.

_____

_____

Continued from page_____

*Continued from page*_____

Continued from page_____

_____

_____

_____

_____

_____

_____

_____

_____

_____

_____

_____

_____

_____

_____

_____

_____

_____

_____

_____

_____

_____   To make it as a writer…
_____   Be prompt.
_____

_____

_____

Continued from page_____

Continued from page_____

*Continued from page*_____

_____

_____

_____

_____

_____

_____

_____

_____

_____

_____

_____

_____

_____

_____

_____

_____

_____

_____

_____

_____

_____   To make it as a writer...

_____   Be prepared.

_____

_____

*Continued from page*_____

Continued from page_____

Continued from page_____

To make it as a writer...
Understand that
hard work makes luck.

Continued from page_____

Continued from page_____

Continued from page_____

To make it as a writer...
Smile, even at times when
you would prefer
a good frown.

Continued from page_____

Continued from page_____

Continued from page_____

To make it as a writer...
Keep fit and be healthy in
mind and spirit.

Continued from page_____

Continued from page_____

Continued from page_____

_____

_____

_____

_____

_____

_____

_____

_____

_____

_____

_____

_____

_____

_____

_____

_____

_____

_____

_____

_____   To make it as a writer...

_____   Become a mentor.

_____

_____

Continued from page_____

Continued from page_____

Continued from page_____

To make it as a writer...
Get the tools you need.

Continued from page_____

Continued from page_____

Continued from page_____

To make it as a writer...
Give compliments.

*Continued from page*_____

Continued from page_____

Continued from page_____

To make it as a writer…
Be generous with praise
and stingy with criticism,
especially with other
emerging writers.

Continued from page_____

_____

_____

_____

_____

_____

_____

_____

_____

_____

_____

_____

_____

_____

_____

_____

_____

_____

_____

_____

_____

_____

_____

_____

_____

_____

_____

_____

_____

_____

_____

Continued from page_____

Continued from page_____

_____

_____

_____

_____

_____

_____

_____

_____

_____

_____

_____

_____

_____

_____

_____

_____

_____

_____

_____

_____

_____

_____

_____   To make it as a writer…
                                          Learn, take classes,
_____   study your craft.

_____

_____

Continued from page_____

Continued from page_____

*Continued from page*_____

To make it as a writer…
Learn the rules
before you break them.

Continued from page_____

*Continued from page*_____

Continued from page_____

_____

_____

_____

_____

_____

_____

_____

_____

_____

_____

_____

_____

_____

_____

_____

_____

_____

_____

To make it as a writer...
Become a resource
for others.

Continued from page_____

Continued from page_____

Continued from page_____

To make it as a writer...
Attend writer's
conferences.

Continued from page_____

*Continued from page*_____

Continued from page_____

To make it as a writer...
Believe in yourself first.

*Continued from page*_____

*Continued from page*_____

Continued from page_____

_____

_____

_____

_____

_____

_____

_____

_____

_____

_____

_____

_____

_____

_____

_____

_____

_____

_____

_____

To make it as a writer...
Work as if everything
depends on you,
but trust as if everything
depends on God.

Continued from page_____

Continued from page_____

Continued from page_____

To make it as a writer...
Visualize the success
you want.

Continued from page_____

*Continued from page*_____

Continued from page_____

To make it as a writer...
Read one book on
creativity every month.

Continued from page_____

Continued from page_____

_____
_____
_____
_____
_____
_____
_____
_____
_____
_____
_____
_____
_____
_____
_____
_____
_____
_____
_____
_____
_____
_____
_____
_____
_____
_____
_____

Continued from page_____

_____

_____

_____

_____

_____

_____

_____

_____

_____

_____

_____

_____

_____

_____

_____

_____

_____

_____

_____

_____   To make it as a writer...

_____   Don't do things that would

_____   embarrass your mom.

*Continued from page*_____

Continued from page_____

Continued from page_____

To make it as a writer...
Be memorable.

Continued from page_____

*Continued from page*_____

*Continued from page*_____

To make it as a writer...
Follow up and then
do it again.

Continued from page_____

Continued from page_____

Continued from page_____

_____

_____

_____

_____

_____

_____

_____

_____

_____

_____

_____

_____

_____

_____

_____

_____

_____

_____

_____

_____

_____

_____

_____

_____   To make it as a writer...

_____   Don't blame others

_____   when it's your fault.

_____

*Continued from page*_____

Continued from page_____

Continued from page_____

_____

_____

_____

_____

_____

_____

_____

_____

_____

_____

_____

_____

_____

_____

_____

_____

_____

_____

To make it as a writer...
Say what you'll do
and do what you say.

*Continued from page*_____

*Continued from page*_____

Continued from page_____

_____

_____

_____

_____

_____

_____

_____

_____

_____

_____

_____

_____

_____

_____

_____

_____

_____

_____

_____

_____

_____   To make it as a writer...
_____   Understand the power
_____   of the question.
_____

Continued from page_____

*Continued from page*_____

Continued from page_____

_____

_____

_____

_____

_____

_____

_____

_____

_____

_____

_____

_____

_____

_____

_____

_____

_____

_____

_____

_____

_____

_____

To make it as a writer...
Don't put down
the competition.

*Continued from page*_____

Continued from page_____

Continued from page_____

_____

_____

_____

_____

_____

_____

_____

_____

_____

_____

_____

_____

_____

_____

_____

_____

_____

_____

_____

_____

To make it as a writer...
Hang around with positive,
successful writers.

Continued from page_____

Continued from page_____

Continued from page_____

_____

_____

_____

_____

_____

_____

_____

_____

_____

_____

_____

_____

_____

_____

_____

_____

_____

_____

_____

To make it as a writer...
Count your blessings.
At least you know the
joy of a creative life.

Continued from page _____

Continued from page_____

*Continued from page*_____

To make it as a writer...
Laugh at yourself.

Continued from page_____

Continued from page_____

Continued from page_____

_____

_____

_____

_____

_____

_____

_____

_____

_____

_____

_____

_____

_____

_____

_____

_____

_____

_____

_____

To make it as a writer...
Find mentors.

*Continued from page*_____

*Continued from page*_____

*Continued from page*_____

To make it as a writer...
Don't keep score.

Continued from page_____

*Continued from page*_____

Continued from page_____

To make it as a writer...
Spend time with yourself.

*Continued from page*_____

*Continued from page*_____

Continued from page_____

Continued from page_____

To make it as a writer...
Develop a strong
work ethic.

Continued from page _____

Continued from page_____

Continued from page_____

To make it as a writer...
Trust others.

Continued from page_____

*Continued from page*_____

_____

_____

_____

_____

_____

_____

_____

_____

_____

_____

_____

_____

_____

_____

_____

_____

_____

_____

_____

_____

_____

_____

_____

_____

_____

_____

_____

_____

*Continued from page*_____

_____

To make it as a writer...
Write.

Here's what they're saying
about your mentor, Eva Shaw:

Rebecca, from Paris, France, writes: If you want encouragement to write well this is the place to find it.

Donna, from La Costa, California, writes: Eva Shaw demystifies creativity and makes it something even the beginning writer can master. With Eva's basic tool kit and steady encouragement, you can learn to joyfully recognize and nurture the creative writer within. That's what she's done for me. —— Donna Marganella, essayist.

Ben, from Pittsburgh, Pennsylvania, writes: I thank you. You hit the bull's eye with me and I do appreciate it very much. I feel the fears have been realized and faced, and I've done it by using your courses and techniques.

Patty, from Los Angeles, California, writes: Thank you for your comments and encouragement regarding my writing. I never expected an online course to be so helpful and really educational.

T., from Dubai, writes: You have shown me not to have any fears when I want to express myself in words, even in words I have never used before. Because of your mentoring, I am sharing my writing and myself with others. Their thoughts and feedback to me are what feeds me as I reach for the peak of my creativity.

Kris, from Perth, Western Australia, writes: Thank you for reaching across the cyber miles to hug and coddle my artist child. I feel so special. I will never forget how marvelous I felt when you first called me "a good writer" and "a dear friend." What a joy!

Lynne, from Phoenix, Arizona, writes: Thanks Eva, for a great class! God bless. Hopefully I'll see you at a conference sometime soon!!!

Ed, from San Antonio, Texas, writes: I thought I was blocked from writing and creativity forever. Thank you for all you have done. I believe we must use the creativity God has given us and yours is a ministry, even if you do make your living at it! Thank you from the bottom of my heart.

Val, from Brooklyn, New York, writes: I am almost in tears. I so enjoyed this course and being a part of it. I'll just have to take another one of Eva's courses. This one got me going and a special thank you, Eva, for making all of the material very down to earth and understandable.

Debbie, from Newark, Delaware, writes: Eva, most of all, I must thank you. You have made it possible for me to participate in something amazing. I knew right from the start that I was going to like you as an instructor. I never thought an online class could be so easy or so fun. You are an incredible teacher and person.

Jack, from Switzerland, writes: You have inspired me to make travel writing my hobby. I have a plan for a travel book on local festivals and I bought your book, Writing the Nonfiction Book, to use as my guide. I will keep all the information from this class to both instruct and inspire me. Thank you for sharing your time and your expertise with me. If you ever travel through this way, let me know so I can have the pleasure of meeting you in person. In other words, "Ya'll come back now, here?"

Norm, from Detroit, Michigan, writes: I don't believe I have ever come across a more encouraging instructor. Thank you for being here when I was.

Tom, from San Jose, California, writes: Dr. Eva, thank you very much for this class. The best compliment I can say to you is I will put everything you taught me to work, and I will put out those queries and stories. I will be in another one of your classes after the summer. In the meantime I am clipping and listening, and one day I will see my essays or articles in print.

Cynthia, from Miami, Florida, writes: Eva, oh, Eva. I can't possibly tell you how much you have influenced me personally and with my writing. Thanks for being such a caring and nurturing teacher. You'll probably "see" me again. Let me know if you're ever in the Fort Lauderdale/Miami area. I would love to share "our" sunrise with you!

Will, from Chula Vista, California, writes: I also feel a bit like I'm graduating and am in fear of losing the support and guidance of my instructor. Chin up. As long as we pursue, perhaps our dreams can become reality.

Kelly Anne, from Boise, Idaho, writes: Eva, you are an inspiration. Thanks for a great class. I wish it would not end. You are the best "writing coach" I have ever had. I know my writing and editing are good, but I didn't have any ideas about how to market my writing. Now I have the material from class, your personalized help, and your book, The Successful Writer's Guide to Publishing Magazine Articles. Now all I have to do is overcome all of the little things (you know those things!) that slow me down whenever I want to write and get published.

Dena, from Idaho Falls, Idaho, writes: Well dah-ling, I took your advice and e-mailed the editor. A few minutes ago I received an e-mail back. "Oh, too soon," I thought, sighing. "It'll be an instant rejection." But wait! She wanted to publish the essay for $150 and said she'll get a contract out today. I am floating on air.

Dottie, from Boulder, Colorado, writes: Thank you, Eva, for all your kind words and encouragement. The class has been a stretch that I've needed for a very long time. You have helped me realize my dreams and this was not an easy task.

Carl, from Lincoln, Nebraska, writes: "Thank you" seems so inadequate, but thank you anyway, Eva, for the confidence, for the encouragement, for everything. I am mind-mapping two different novel ideas based on prairie life. Who knows what will come of it, nothing more than self-fulfillment and that will be o.k. I have rediscovered a passion, something that brings me satisfaction and joy. I just stumbled onto this course through a local college advertisement, but then we both know the Lord moves in mysterious ways. We shall meet again, my friend. Perhaps this fall, when I have completed the reading list that accompanied these first twelve lessons! I wish you continued good health and good fortunes.

GG, from Anchorage, Alaska, writes: Going against our beloved instructor's advice, I showed my spouse a copy of an essay and asked for his opinion, since I needed to send it to the editor pronto. He shrugged, "It's okay. Not great, but okay." Arrow to the heart. I went with my instincts and sent it anyway. I am getting ready to call him at work with a mature comment such as, "Nyay-nyah-nyay-nyay, Nyay." It's a compliment to you that my first thought was, "I have to get online and tell Eva." Repercussions to the husband come second.

Gemma, from Perth, Australia, writes: Eva, I have enjoyed this class more than I have enjoyed anything since my kids were still home. I guess I will have to adopt a new hobby and write more often. I think more than writing, I enjoyed the interaction of fellow novices. This class wouldn't be the same if you were any different. Thank you for being you! I intend to take the other three classes you offer this year so you haven't heard the last of me.

Anne, from Kansas City, Missouri, writes: I feel a total let down now that the class is over. I'll miss you, but I'll be back in class again, the good Lord willing and the creek don't rise.

Susan, from Irvine, California writes: Never question if you have made a difference in someone's life. You have.

Rita, from White Plains, New York, writes: You've listened to my dreams of becoming a published writer from the first moment I "walked" into class, and you believed me so I believed me. Now it's true. I've sold articles and essays. I'm on my way. Thank you for nudging and the creative exercises. Thanks for your positive and encouraging attitude.

Corky, from Eau Claire, Wisconsin, writes: If anyone had told me that in six short weeks I'd change from would-be writer to published magazine writer — using an online class with an instructor 2,000 miles away — I would have laughed myself silly. But it's true, thanks to you, Eva.

Pushpa, from Scranton, Pennsylvania, writes: Eva, I have really enjoyed this class. It brought a lot of excitement in my life. Talk about my passions. Now all I do is think about writing. So many ideas flowing through my mind and now I do find time to put them to paper. Thank you for all the inspiring words and the encouragement you have provided through the course. I am actually going to print the discussion notes from all of you for future encouragement. Thanks again. Good luck with your new book with creativity exercises.

Linda, from Laguna Nigel, California, writes: I have three articles in the works that I think are winners. I don't have the query yet, but I will soon. More important, I won't be nervous about pitching it, since I know I can do it fast and competently, thanks to the mentoring you've given me. I'm thrilled with the course and optimistic about magazine writing.

Karen, from Pasadena, California, writes: Thanks so much for the clear, informative, and practical class! I enjoyed it immensely. Last week a magazine contacted me interested in my heirloom gardening query. Pretty exciting news. Thanks so much for the extra push to get me out there in the writing world instead of just reading and dreaming.

Kari, from Fort William, Ontario, Canada, writes: A note to budding writers: Six months ago (pre-Eva days) I was "just" a stay at home mum. Today I received my first contract for a magazine article. Many thanks, Eva, for helping me, not only to understand techniques of writing, but, more importantly, for helping me realize a hitherto dream.

MN, from Huntsville, Alabama, writes: Thank you, Eva . Your class got me writing again instead of thinking about it. The weeks flew by. I've sold one article to our newspaper and I've just put ten queries in the mail. I couldn't have done it without you, my dear mentor.

Bruce, from Oakland, California, writes: Eva, thanks for your encouraging remarks. I'm glad you enjoyed the essay I've just finished. I felt pretty good about it. When I read it to my wife and daughter, they cried, which excited me because it elicited the response I was hoping for. I can't thank you enough for your professional training and sincere encouragement. Rather than enrolling in another of your excellent courses, I will now concentrate on actually "doing something" with my creations.

Christy, from Moreno Valley, California, writes: If you buy only one creative writing book — buy this one. Synonymous with creativity and writing genius, Eva strips away the mysteries of the writing universe. Brimming with creative possibility, this book is a must-have for seasoned or aspiring writers everywhere. — Christy Selter, freelance writer

Marilee, from Danbury, Connecticut, writes: I have thought about writing seriously for several years, but it wasn't until I took your classes that I actually wrote anything. You have helped me realize my dream.

ORDERING INFORMATION

QTY	ITEM DESCRIPTION	UNIT PRICE	TOTAL PRICE
	Shovel It: Nature's Health Plan	$15.95	
	Publishing Magazine Articles	$15.95	
	Writing the Nonfiction Book	$18.95	
	Writeriffic: Creativity Training for Writers	$14.95	

CREDIT CARD INFORMATION

For credit card orders call our toll-free number OR send order form and credit card information to:

Writeriffic Publishing Group
P.O. Box 524
Carlsbad, CA 92018-0524
Toll-free: 866-244-9047 or FAX to: 760-729-1326

❏ **Visa** ❏ **MasterCard** ❏ **American Express** ❏ **Discover**

Name on card: _____

Card Number: _____ Expiration Date: _____

TOTAL	
SHIPPING* ADD $3.50 PER BOOK	
CA RESIDENTS ADD 7.5% SALES TAX	
TOTAL ORDER	

* For orders outside of the
  U.S., please contact
  Writeriffic Publishing Group

SHIPPING ADDRESS

Mr./Mrs./Ms._____

Address_____

City _____ State _____ Zip _____

Phone#   Day (___)_____   Eve. (___)_____

E-Mail address: _____
Fill in ONLY if you want to receive SPECIAL OFFERS

PERSONAL AUTOGRAPH INFORMATION

_____

_____

_____